THE SEIZURE OF THE BEAST.

A POST-RESEARCH.

GUERNICA WORLD EDITIONS 69

IULIA MILITARU

THE SEIZURE OF THE BEAST.

A POST-RESEARCH.

Translated from the Romanian
by Claudia Serea

TORONTO—CHICAGO—BUFFALO—LANCASTER (U.K.)

2023

Guernica Editions Founder: Antonio D'Alfonso

Michael Mirolla, editor
Cover and interior design: Errol F. Richardson

Guernica Editions Inc.
287 Templemead Drive, Hamilton (ON), Canada L8W 2W4
2250 Military Road, Tonawanda, N.Y. 14150-6000 U.S.A.
www.guernicaeditions.com

Distributors:
Independent Publishers Group (IPG)
600 North Pulaski Road, Chicago IL 60624
University of Toronto Press Distribution (UTP)
5201 Dufferin Street, Toronto (ON), Canada M3H 5T8

First edition.
Printed in Canada.

Legal Deposit—Third Quarter
Library of Congress Catalog Card Number: 2023938118
Library and Archives Canada Cataloguing in Publication
Title: *The seizure of the beast : a post-research* / Iulia Militaru ; translated from the Romanian
by Claudia Serea.
Other titles: *Confiscarea bestiei*. English
Names: Militaru, Iulia, author. | Serea, Claudia, translator.
Series: Guernica world editions (Series) ; 69.
Description: Series statement: Guernica world editions ; 69 | Poems. | Translation of:
Confiscarea bestiei.
Identifiers: Canadiana 20230448720 | ISBN 9781771838481 (softcover)
Classification: LCC PC840.423.I72 C6613 2023 | DDC 859/.135—dc23

The Seizure of the Beast.
A Post-research.

Concept and work method

THIS BOOK IS THE result of a several-years-long research on the phenomenon of alienation and the process of becoming. From the onset, its concept used an experimental technique of taking over certain archived objects (concepts) and recycling them, thus building a *repertoire* that places the book in the realm of performative writing. My purpose was to use as literary speech "the feeling" of concepts used in various fields dealing with the vast theme of alienation. The experiment focused on determining the affective potential of speeches invested with an "objective authority"—especially the scientific discourse. My method consisted of combining various types of speech, taken from different fields, using noncreative writing as a main technique against representation. I wanted to present these speeches directly, without any associated commentary or analysis. The literary discourse is also included in this experiment to track the effects of introducing an emotional element in a rational construct.

At its core, the book has the nucleus-concept of undecidability as a trait of the Other and as a possibility to maintain an open future by keeping open the meaning—as Yasmin Gunaratnam said, "a temporal and ethical relationship" ("a meaning that calls attention to the precarious and creative condition in which interpretation takes place"—see the poem "The Purpose of the Post-research"). This undecidability is in permanent danger of being "violated" by attributing to it a meaning dependent of a fictional context (a context declared as fixed and that generates a unique, absolute meaning). In this experiment, the nucleus-concept and the fictional context are the two elements generating the potential emotion. By associating the archived objects with new contexts and interpretations, the performative component of writing is activated.

The essay-poem has "the waiting living being" as a main character made visible by the absolute deprivation of the environment which ensures its survival. The text also becomes a presentation of the form that zoé (the bare-life) can assume and its relationship with death and the representations of the "living". If in nature the possibility of bare-life inception depends on the conditions created by nature for its diversity of species in various climates, in the case of human society, history is what determines the changes and creates the extreme environment in which the bare-life becomes visible. Thus, the two take on an identical function, resulting in the possibility of erasing the distinction between history and nature, history becoming only one of the conditions that nature creates for the human species. The visible result of "the waiting living being" is the terrifying image of the non-human anthropophagous being, the cannibal or the savage, the Other or the beast. These are the images generated by the undecidability of the Other when "violated"—and the same ones I tried deconstructing. If the living body can act not only through a conscientious decision, but also through indeterminacy (see Elisabeth Grosz), this means that a series of events are produced independently of any rational control, and the speeches representing them are nothing but an attempt to "violate" the undecidability. "The act once performed, once actualized, is different from the indeterminacy of its performance" (Elisabeth Grosz). In consequence, through performative and noncreative writing, the speech is given back to indeterminacy; in its potential and renewed state, the speech generates the difference through which the relationship with the Other continues to remain open, thus the relationship with the older representations becomes fluid. This is only possible through the act.

—*Iulia Militaru, translated by Claudia Serea*

This is not a poem

Euclid, when he finished *The Elements*, thought he created Geometry—but he had only written a new fantasy literary work.
—**Alberto Mussa,** *The Balance of the Pendulum*

Problem: Is this still a poem?

1ˢᵗ Strophe: Anyone can answer, reading between the lines: indeed, this is not a poem because we know what a poem is! So, no need to explain, and explaining wouldn't make sense. No one ever thought the following text could be poetry.

1ˢᵗ Antistrophe: Your title is inept! Sirs, bowing with humility in front of those who know, I'd say that, truthfully, when I wrote this, I had no idea what it is. Then, I said to myself, even Magritte's pipe is not a pipe although it is one.

2ⁿᵈ Strophe: But, about the pipe, although we certainly know it is a pipe, Magritte had the guts to throw this into the faces of the ones who knew: No, this is not a pipe, you have no clue.

2ⁿᵈ Antistrophe: And, ultimately, what is a pipe? A physical object? An image? A simple word?

3ʳᵈ Strophe: The pipe is the word that can be used to name a physical object used in the action known as smoking. In order to link the action to the word pipe, we need the preposition "to."

3ʳᵈ Antistrophe: Therefore: What are we using the pipe for? To smoke!

4ᵗʰ Strophe: There are certain gestures always associated with the aforementioned action. Because of them, the action occurs. And these gestures have in turn action names: to stuff, to light, to move, to redden, to inhale, to press, to smoke, to re-light, to wipe, to cool, to clean. A noun always used in the context of the pipe is the tobacco. You've read a lot about it because a lot has been said. So, we know what the tobacco is, but we're not interested in it because no one had the courage to deny its existence.

4ᵗʰ Antistrophe: Will there ever be born a Magritte of the tobacco?

5th Strophe: Let's get back to the pipe and to the poem. In conclusion, all the objects used as described above exist under the pipe name, if they weren't destroyed. A few ways to destroy them can actually be presented: through hitting, throwing, ripping, cutting, etc. As a result, only the pieces remain of what was once a pipe, about which we can't say it is a pipe any longer.

5th Antistrophe: But let's not stop now, let's continue thinking! Is the case of the poem analogue to the one of the pipe? What do we use the poem for and how do we use poetry? Are there any objects used as poetry after they were destroyed?

The poem:
We use it to show off our genius to the individuals of the opposite sex.
We use it to guide our spirit toward dreaming.
We use it to escape reality.
We use it to dive into reality.
To change the world.
To preserve the world.
To forget.
To remember.
For everything.
For nothing.

The poem:
Is written on a white sheet, printed between book covers, or copied into a notebook, sometimes you can see it painted on the walls of various buildings, preferably in public toilets. It's often used recited, memorized, read, or ignored.

The poem:
Is frequently used together with adjectives such as: beautiful, sublime, sensitive, ineffable, infinite, damned, cursed, genius, reflexive.
But also, banal, common, quotidian, jaded, genital, transitive.
Or conceptual, rational, void, empty, experimental, etc.

The poem:
Appears in structures next to abyss, dream, ireality, being, non-being.
Or city, street, mizerabilism, body, blood, bones.
or void, nothing, experiment, Wittgenstein, Deleuze.

Epode 1: The word "authentic" in any context is a must.

If you destroy the objects from the first category, the ones from the second category appear.
If you destroy the objects from the second category, the ones from the third category appear.
If you destroy the objects from the third category, the ones from the first two categories appear.
Thus, the remains of the destroyed objects formerly known as poems are often called poetry. This is the main difference from the pipe object.

This demonstrates the following: the poem can be used anywhere; the poem can be used any way. The poem can be destroyed, the poem cannot be destroyed. The poem is unique, the poem is recyclable, etc.

Epode 2: Therefore, "This is not a poem" is a poem that is not a poem. *But we must be silent about the things we cannot speak about.*

Despite this, you know what a poem is! So, speak!

Post-research: is this still a poem?

This is not a poem.
It's not an anti-poem, either.

It's an attempt to establish
the anatomical sex and sexual
identity of a concept around which
your existence rotates:
From the right to the left,
from the left to the right;

from the left to the left,
from the right to the right;

And so on, or maybe otherwise,
until the poem is dizzy, the idiot.

Death   the cessation of the vital processes at the organs and
                    tissue level
        the state in which the central nervous system shows
                    irreversible lesions
        when resuscitation is not possible any longer
        death occurs, as in the end of life.

Death   simple common noun, singular, feminine gender

Any evil   thing
            received through language
Is of a   feminine gender

This is the beauty of languages with gender terminations!

life?	feminine	is evil
death?	feminine	is evil
survival?	feminine	is evil
suicide?	feminine	is evil

But the gender can become neutral. Ultimately:

evil?	neutral	indefinite

The purpose of the post-research

What we're interested in is the point at which the words can be
confiscated
or the small tear of the hymen between:
living/nonliving   masculine/feminine
I/someone

Then and only then when they appear:
semantic confusions
linguistic violence
permanent revolutions

All in their impossibility u(n/m)(d/b)eci(dabi)lity

The definition of a term necessary to the post-demonstration: The fugue

Through fugue, or run, we usually understand:
Either moving with big, fast steps,
or leaving a place in a hurry
　　　to escape a constraint or a danger.
There is also the exceptional meaning of the fugue,
Polyphonic musical form with two or more voices,
　　　in which the melody played by one voice is repeated in turn
　　　and developed by the other voices according to the counterpoint laws.
And also, the unusual meaning: fugue and death,
a case of partial synonymy between two
simple common nouns of feminine gender.

For poetry and its readers,
however free they think they are,
only the unusual and the exceptional meanings
　　　will always matter.
Everything else disappears in the amorphous mass
　　　of usual presences
　　　and ordinary catachreses.

Fugue and death　　　　　two words
different meanings　　　　common language

Demise,
liberating stimulations of the matter.

Crying,
hypertrophied lacrimal glands.

This is how things should go,
nothing abnormal, nothing strange.

And yet,
Dacians were laughing at funerals,
nothing abnormal, nothing strange.
Laughter stimulates endogenous endorphins
and reduces the risk of cancer.

But paradox follows the human being.

Death caused by too much laughter is both a particular and exceptional situation. Usually, it occurs through cardio-respiratory stoppage. From antiquity to present day, many cases of killer laughter have been recorded. More information here:
http://filosofiatis.blogspot.ro/2014/12/ars-moriendi.html

Physiopathology: Numerous problems of the human anatomy and physiology transform the benign laughter into a ferocious killer. Thus, lesions of the brain stem, of the bridge of Varolio, and of the medulla can trigger pathological laughter, causing atony and syncope, followed by other lesions, such as those of the hypothalamus. These can extend to the cerebellum.

Epode: Emotional lability is just a simple sign of the predisposition to death by laughter/ never a cause of it.

Dying (of laughter) is no joke!

Death: What is free of your intentions/What always occurs outward; Reprehensible when it becomes your intention/Reprehensible when it doesn't occur outwardly.

      The perfect model of decentralizing,
        losing the head, the absolute freedom of the body:

1. the myocardium remains excitable for 15-20 minutes;
2. muscular fibers keep their excitability for 5-6 hours;
3. the pupil can be stimulated
(by subconjunctival injection of Atropine or Pilocarpine, for 4-6 hours);
4. the cilia from the respiratory epithelium keep their mobility for 12/24/36 hours;
5. spermatozoa keep their mobility for 72 hours.

These are the supravital manifestations,
in other words, all that is above life.

A supreme anticapitalist gesture, the gathering of capital.

      Facial hair and nails grow anarchically,
      the intestines live for the first time
      the miracle of unconditional liberation
      from the accumulated gas. Flatulence,
      the moment of great personal freedom

Death can be sold and bought on the black market for a minimum price. Negotiation is allowed only outside the accredited institutions where the price is fixed and mandated by the State.

Death—not at all a sudden occurrence, but a dynamic process with variable length in which the vital systems of the body participate simultaneously or in sequence and which results in the demise of the individual. This process is influenced by the variable response of the cells to diminishing quantities of oxygen and nutrients.

Early signs: the cooling of the body, dehydration, autolysis, deathly pallor, rigor mortis.
Later signs: destructive changes caused by animals, insects, rot;
Preserving changes (through mummification, lignification, freezing, mineralization)

[**Did you know** ... that recently, it was discovered that the dead don't rot any longer:

1ˢᵗ Voice: "For 20 years since I've been working as a grave digger here, I found many mummified bodies. We find one every 2-3 weeks. I remember about a month ago, when we had to dig up someone, we found a lady perfectly mummified. Her face skin was stretched, teeth in their places, even her clothes were in good condition. When we dug her out of the grave and held her up, she stood as if she were alive".

2ⁿᵈ Voice: "Lately, the gravediggers find more and more mummified bodies when they exhume the ones dead for over 7 years. Some say it's God's miracle, others say the tombs are to blame because they're sealed and don't allow bacteria to decompose the body. The researchers say the bodies don't "properly" rot any longer because of the preservatives and additives from the food we eat daily."

All of these signs were recently graded.
No one ever believed there is a death Law,
(let alone, a definition of it; only images)
One could die and live as they pleased:

1. Suicide by firearm, September 20, 1890, female; the following note was found: *Beloved Vasile, if you'd like to do me a last favor, please pay the washerwoman 7 lei and 50 bani; I wouldn't want her to curse my soul; and to the kerosene seller I must pay 1 leu and 75 bani; if you want, ask the French woman or the maid to pay him. Please don't deny me my last wish. And one more thing. Please, I'm asking you, when I'm dead, show some interest in me, do something, anything you want, to show you're sorry, or do what you know, but do it so the world can see. You know very well this is not for me, because I won't know anything; but for you, because there are some people who know my entanglement and they will gossip a lot behind your back. They are already, even without this. Please, listen to me, do something to save your reputation, something that wouldn't cost you money you don't have. Please listen, I know what I'm saying. Forgive me for giving you advice, it's because I don't want you to have any troubles because of me. Kisses!*

2. Suicide by poisoning with phenic acid, November 21, 1890, male; the following note was found: *Look, I'm drinking phenic acid; I'm poisoning myself!*

3. Suicide by poisoning with arsenic, December 11, 1898, unspecified sex; no note was found; in the morgue archive's log, one can read: *He didn't say he was sick with anything; but for a while this person was very sad.*

More abuse occurred.
Denying death, overvaluing life,
the absence of a clear explanation for
being alive.

Lastly, the ultimate confusion.

Epode: They resorted to SCIENTIFIC/research.

Th(a/o)[u/n](a)tology: The study of all aspects related to death/Is called thanatology.

The experiments were developed
in several stages:

1. Decorporalization (exiting the body, perceiving events that occur farther away from the individual)
2. Increasingly fast aspiration through a tunnel at the end of which one can see an intense but gentle light; along the way, the individual replays the entire life.
3. Before merging with the light source, the individual returns to his/her body (the return is extremely unpleasant)

The results were analyzed,
solid counterarguments were made
against the proof of "after life" existence:

- *The existence of a universal hallucination prototype, regardless of cause (tiredness, fever, epilepsy, drugs, sensory deprivation).*
- *Very similar phenomena can occur through electrostimulation of the temporal lobe in the fissure of Sylvius or through administering ketamine, phencyclidine, or LSD.*
- *It's possible that these sensations are caused by massive endorphins production.*

A law, to regulate this aspect,
toxic for any developed society, was necessary.

Elaboration: A few capable individuals were needed.
They gathered two-three words,
Placed them in a certain order,
Constructing meaning. Then, they priced it.

1ˢᵗ Epode: So any Law can be/is sold. The one who doesn't own a
Law should buy one!

This is the role of the parliament: to sell us overpriced laws,
otherwise known and accepted by the citizens as a parliamentary salary.

A law can be good or bad. To select the good ones,
fit for commercial purpose, we need a president.
His advice cost also a considerable amount of money.

The process of selling and buying laws is called democracy.
For this, democracy is not necessary; only the capitalist spirit is necessary.

2ⁿᵈ Epode: Any spirit can in turn be/is sold.
The one who doesn't have a spirit should buy one!

Commercial break/time rotation:

Because the SPIRIT is your guardian,
any herd (of well-tempered domestic animals), in its absence, is vulnerable.

He, known as the shepherd,
"accepts to take on his shoulders the animals' sins, so they don't have to
pay a price";
the shepherd will be the one who pays a price,
instead of you. This is the advantage of being shepherded!

Results: According to the Law, it was established that:
Total death = the end of activity of all the body cells

The Law's contradictions:
It's not clear if "death" means:
1. cardiac activity arrest (?)
2. the irreversible destruction of the brain (?)

Positive diagnostic of cerebral death:
1. complete loss of relation life
2. total muscular areflexia and atonia
3. BP drop when the iatrogenous support is cut off
4. spontaneous respiration stop
5. persistent electrical "quiet" on the EEG

There are people that can stay in a vegetative state several years and who spontaneously recover their cerebral activity.
Because of the existence of cerebral death, the confusion between living and non-living persists, which makes applying the law difficult.

Several amendments were necessary.

Exclusions from the "Living" category after imposing the definition and establishing the death legislation

So far, we don't have all the necessary approvals to cite a complete list.

On the short list, there are noted only:

1. The category of the one who believes himself the father of the next two categories, proudly calling himself "the author"; at this one, it was observed, in time, the presence of the signs necessary to maintain the diagnostic of cerebral death, in other words, of the irreversible destruction of the brain: first and foremost, the complete loss of relation life, areflexia, and the persistent electrical "quiet" on the EEG.

2. The category of the one that history thought inoffensive up to a point, but was wrong: "the reader"; his death through cardiac arrest was necessary. Besides the cooling of the body, lividity, and rigor mortis, he started to show destructive changes caused by insects and rot. Each reader has a specific stench. But miraculously, it was observed that the spermatozoa retained their mobility, in this type of body, even after more than 72 hours since death. Thus, the reproductive function continues to develop well. So far, science didn't plausibly explain this phenomenon.

3. The "poem" category: with ambiguous signals from this category, such as, firstly, the absence of a deceased body, it is believed the poem has been hiding in a vegetative state for several years, and everyone is feverishly awaiting its spontaneous revival.

Epode: It's worth mentioning the fact that none of the excluded categories is definitely excluded.

Exclusion oscillates depending on the historic period and context. *Everything is relative.*

Additional specifications regarding death

If interested in the faith of its members, society will be announced of their death through an obituary published in the pages of the local papers.

A beautiful homage, sometimes touching, demonstrates everyone's interest at a very low price. Following are a few examples of such obituaries, copied from the journal of my grandfather, Ion Popescu:

1. Toward the end of March 1953, Joseph Vissarionovich Stalin (aged approx. 73 years) passed away. At that time, our country kept three days of mourning, and church bells rang everywhere for him. That's when I heard that many party members were confused by the bells, since communists are atheists and don't believe in God.

2. In the year 1978, I found out from the newspaper România Liberă that reserve colonel Elefterescu Juarez has passed. I went to his funeral at the Resurrection cemetery where I met several reserve officers that I knew and spent some time talking with them. Still from the newspaper România Liberă I found out that have passed:

> ** Barat Israel (Liviu), former major and my boss at the M.I.A.[1];*
> ** Onviceanu Emil, former chief of the fridge shop at the Repairs Group*
> ** Bârlădeanu Vasile, former colleague of mine at the Endowments Ministry.*

3. In the newspaper România Liberă from May 14, 1978, they announced the sudden passing of the singer from Dâmbovița County, Ileana Sărăroiu. She was buried on Wednesday, May 16, at the Sfânta Vineri cemetery.

---

[1]M.I.A.= Ministry of Internal Affairs

4. In the newspaper Flacăra from September 13, 1979, no.37, a very important article was published: "The Ranitescu Inheritance", by dr. res. col. Ranitescu Dumitru, deceased on September 2, 1979 (operated in July 1979). He had created the product D.R. that cures a series of cancerous diseases. Death occurred through an accident not yet explained (under investigation); (text written by Emanoil Valeriu).

5. On Sunday, February 22, 1981 reserve colonel Bârsășeanu Cristache was buried at the Crângași cemetery. I couldn't attend because I went to the public bath in Giulești.

6. In the newspaper România Liberă from November 12, 1986, it was announced that Viceslav Molotov, former politician in Stalin's time, has died at 96 years of age.

7. Tuesday, January 13, 1987, three years since Edi's death, Rica kept a requiem at the cemetery. She also paid for an obit in the newspaper România Liberă in which it was written: On January 13, three years since the sudden stop of the thread of many happy years, when I lost forever the wise, kind, and honorable man, engineer Eduard Rădulescu, former director in the Labor Ministry. Now I know only the pain, longing, and the suffering of terrible loneliness until the end of my life. —Wife Maria

8. Tuesday, June 23, 1987, it was published in the newspaper România Liberă that colonel engineer Nedeianu Jakues, who was my boss at the Construction Service from the M.I.A., has died. When I retired on March 1, 1977, he sent his secretary to buy for me: a robe, a pair of slippers, and a bottle of wine of the best quality. I was sorry I couldn't go to the funeral.

9. In the România Liberă newspaper from Friday, July 10, 1987, it was published that father Munteanu from the Crângași church has died, and in the paper România Liberă from July 14, 1987, it was published that colonel in reserve Ursache Dumitru, who worked with me at the M.I.A., has died.

10. In the România Liberă newspaper from July 30, 1987, it was published that Gheorghe Petrescu, great statesman, the brother of Elena Ceaușescu, born in May 1915 in the village of Petrești, Dâmbovița county, has died. In the same newspaper, it was published that army general Ion Ioniță, aged 64, has died.

Epilogue

after Anemone Latzina

Dear Anemone, don't give up!

As for him …

He broke countless windows, exhausted by too much patience
and tasted hungrily from your bodies, like a hyena.

Alone, he surrounded himself with thick walls, so you can't watch him.
But one morning, he found himself in your orchard full of fruits.

He sent several people to their death while they were kissing his body,
so joyously, as no one ever was.

Then he made love in the sea, despite its coldness,
he made love there, until four blond children were born.

Now, drunk on too much absinthe, he looks to the end of all five,
Killed by life's small illusions he weaves impatiently for them.

He desired the pleasant drug sweetness each day,
and, in this dream, he replanted the scented date trees from your garden.

He won ten medals for this, plus countless riches,
then, he started shooting cats with golden bullets.

Sometimes, he danced the polonaise so well in your arms,
But, unknowingly, he fell in love on May 13 and forgot.

Suddenly, he saw himself inside, and the ones outside returned.
Sometime, maybe by accident, I'll commit suicide, as well.

Laughing.

But … what is important is the end of a form[1].
The freer you are, there is only suicide, even when
your death is declared to have occurred by natural causes.

Now you understand the Werther effect?

DEATH – *the condition of life progress!*

---

[1]The bodies can be: buried (in soil, in caves, in tree hollows, in funeral wells, in monumental graves), incinerated, exposed to open air, thrown into rivers, or eaten in ritualic endocanibalism, etc.

Conversions

She liked it when I whipped her well.
So, she could feel it, immobilized in the tight chains that wounded her,
for these voluptuous punishments were lightening her conscience.
They chased away any feeling of culpability.
    —Alain Robbe-Grillet

Sad-ism

Iustina came my way with/without a body,
stepping slowly on pain in/without place.
I was left without HATE, people, let's stand in line to get and hate
the one before us,
hate him and kill him in terrible torture,
wordless,
people, let's treat Iustina for her sickness, without her silence
I look at her profile, the way light slides on her bare back,
a veil of sorts,
                    BRILLIANT.
Her bare foot
fleshless, stepped slowly on pain. Turning the cave wheel with her
helplessness, painting red my whip with frozen blood
and I hit hard
and I hit to hurt,
merciless. Let's cure Iustina of her sickness. Anyone can win this right
for only 39,90 lei.

Her silence is borne lightly,
                    whispering inside us,
and grows over that cursed place, over the castle on the mountaintop,
over the terrifying ravine,
when I crush her livid body
                            matching so well
the snow
                in that cold year like animal stillness,
white snowflakes adorn an innocent forehead
                        and the entire splendor gathers in her
translucent womb, torn apart, through which I see her small-lit
vagina, frenetically pulsing with each hit it takes,
shameless,
        from Iustina's pain, it lives on my lust.

In that cold, still year,
useless ...

It was allowed for her to be oppressed —
only to overcome her in Heavens with the most flattering riches,
only to shower us on earth with the most delightful gifts.

Spaces

She sits
                    A big dirty metallic table, she's dead,
her most beautiful body,
naked and cold in the sharp light

Translucent pyramids.
The city rests, drawn, through the lines, signs, and gazes. Here.
Me[1]. Now. Its power lies in this dynamic flux.

Calm,
                    she looks toward the holy and deaf mother-of-pearl
glass
the most beautiful body,
hers and only hears, shines everywhere.

And brings her peace.
From her body, thousands of wires start toward the thousands of
screens everywhere. Only her smile comes back. Justina is protected,
only her, anytime, anywhere. *Who wouldn't give her entire life for this?*

---

[1]Marin: "The portrait is a model in epistemological sense, but it is also what is put in the place of
... instead of ... what is substituted for ... In portrait the trait, the line drawn, refers us back to the
trace, vestige, remainder, or ruin, but also to the drawing that is a design, and, in the final analysis,
to the project."

Jamming: Your online identity is built upon the content of your posts on social media. These, together with the other interactions you have online, make up your personal data. Starting here, the button on the bottom of the navigation page will help you, by simply clicking it, to redefine yourself. A simple click and the button will select certain activities in your place. By using it, you'll be able to mask and reconstitute your image by changing the algorithms that recognize you. For more information, read below!

1st Text: "The author is part of the structure of the work. While our modern culture is concerned with the legalities of ownership and appropriation, historically, discourse was an action, not a property. The concept of an author is socially constructed and exists only in relationship to the text. [...] There is not one authorial voice in the text but many as others interpret the discourse from multiple perspectives and add, delete, and otherwise modify the meme to reflect these myriad interpretations."

2nd Text: "Traditional ideas about identity have been tied to the notion of authenticity that such virtual experiences actively subvert. When each player can create many characters and participate in many games, the self is not only decentered but multiplied without limit."

3rd Text: "In this view, the self is not even contained in the body, but can also be realized through relationship with technology. Notions of presence and absence are based in the idea of the body as a center of control and being, but technology is revising this paradigm."

Epode: "To you, the ones who were before me, or come after me, I'm gifting you this space!"

Rules for using this space:

1. Thou shalt have no other spaces before me.
2. Thou shalt not make unto thee any graven image. Thou shalt not worship other spaces.
3. Thou shalt not take the name of this space in vain.
4. Thou shalt work tirelessly for this space, in all the days spent here.
5. Renounce thy father and thy mother, for you only belong to this space. No one outside it can have you.
6. Thou shalt kill the trespassers, lest they worship this space.
7. Thou shalt fornicate! Fornication will take away your inner desert. Build on me!
8. Thou shalt steal from outside and bring all riches here. Thou shalt prosper and breed in my name, merciless, boundless, moral-less! Everything you like you should store here, don't leave anything out.
9. Thou shalt lie in every moment of your presence here. Shout to them: everything is mine!
10. Thou shalt covet the goods that are not yours. Only through them you can make me bigger.

Breaking the above laws will be punished by the maximum sentence, except for the individuals who will pay in its integrity within five days the sum listed in the contract attached to the legislative packet.

About the sense of ownership

All these laws that you were taught today you must guard, so you can live and multiply, and inherit this space. For I am the one who shields you from the surrounding desert. Listen to me!

"Thou shalt not add anything to what has been ordered." Not one word added or subtracted thou tongue shall utter.

This space shall smother from you any other spaces, little by little: "One can't lose them quickly, for the land will go bare and the wild animals will breed against you."

For I am the earth into which you pass to be shepherded, a country with mountains and valleys and waters from the Heaven's rain.

I will chase away all the other spaces in front of you and you'll own greater and stronger spaces than you.

But heed my word, thou shall eat only blood, because the blood carries life and you will eat life together with the flesh.

And thou shalt eat the fruit of your womb, the flesh of your sons and daughters, if you desire this space. Your men will not share with anyone the flesh of their children, which they'll keep only for themselves. Your women will watch with merciless eyes their men and sons and daughters,

and they will not relinquish the newborn who was born through their thighs and the children they gave birth to, because they will eat them in secret during the siege and the famine begotten in my name. Thou shalt survive me!

Rewrite/Description/Streak:

One of the fundamental duties of the State is to streak the space that it owns or use the smooth spaces as means of communication at the service of the streaked space.

This book presents in a succinct way the general principles of a job well done, regardless of the field in which the human activities take place. The author insists on the fact that the t(a/o)[u/n](a)tology she systematically presents is a generalization of the principles of economic science, that th(a/o)[u/n](a)tology is a meta-theory of the economy. Considering the fact that economic science concerns itself, among other things, with optimizing the connections between different specific activities, one could propose the following hierarchy: the th(a/o)[u/n](a)tology generalizes the optimizing principles of the economy, and in turn, this gives directions to optimize the "technical" activities in their widest meaning.

Any and only the act that doesn't achieve its purpose, nor makes it possible or easier to achieve it, in other words, that doesn't get it closer to the purpose, is deemed inefficient. Among inefficient acts there are on one hand anti-efficient acts that render null or make it difficult to attain the purpose, and on the other hand the acts that aren't efficient nor anti efficient but indifferent.

Efficiency and anti-efficiency are gradable; only indifference can't be graded.

The skeleton of the th(a/o)[u/n](a)tology is built on some rules of the efficient activity such as: the economy of actions, preparing them, tooling, integration, or cooperation. One of the most common ways of achieving an economy of the actions is automation, which consists in replacing the intensive actions with machine actions. That which was done conscientiously and with difficulty is now done without thoughts being concentrated on the action. Such manipulative efficiency can be achieved only through experience.

An action, in order to be efficient, needs to be prepared by making a plan that has to contain a well-defined purpose and cover a timeline as long as possible toward the future. A correct plan has to be especially a finalized one that leads realistically to the desired goal without taking us on the wrong paths.

Tooling is the third rule of an efficient action. By using good quality tools, we often achieve an action of incomparable greater safety and precision then by direct manipulation. With the help of tools, we can create many products with such likeness to one another that they can replace each other.

But about space
                we can only talk
outside the space;
where the field goats roam, light-footed,
                and the wood locks fan over the earth;

                where the sun penetrates the grass, leaving it pregnant,
and Juliet enjoys herself with minotaurs, gods, and meads.

Double epode: With our gods, full of fruits/Juliet is wasting her life,
in the grass, pregnant with sun

and trembles when she sees her face/in their large eyes on the horizon
in the grass pregnant with sun.

Her body under pleasures, Juliet suddenly meets her eyes:
                everywhere
                        only Iustina's eyes[1].

And rushing, a line
turning into death/a line of destruction
pure and simple.

---

[1] "The shepherd is the one who keeps watch" over the flock and "will guard the smallest animal from the flock against the danger". A healthy flock is one that produces quality individuals, able to consume and be consumed.

Let's not forget!

If people really understood my painting, it would
mean the end of state capitalism and totalitarianism.
 —Barnett Newman

Prolegomenon: the power/ speech-image as text agony

Promenade

1.

And any journey starts this way, by someone asking:
Why would you want to go there again?

The traces get lost in the road dust,
the boots follow them to the end
next to the endless brick mountains,
the last remains of some graves.

The smell of the ghosts still asleep and a few
butterflies in the dry ashes of the ground.

In the women's section, the tourists
enter in the barrack #26. An old woman
walks among the wooden platforms,
stops, searches with her gaze, she shows us …
"Look, my bed was there"[1].

Then, piles of clothes and the windows
with the hair of the dead. The hair resists. The hair.
It can be reused. Here are the products
made from that hair. Behind
the glass. In front of it, a woman dressed in bright
red. Has a picture taken with the remains.

The photo is the only testimonial.
The ones interested can find it on Facebook,
as a profile picture of a lady dressed in
b/right red.

---

[1] Adapted from a poem by Linda Ashear, b. 1941

2.

Still, it was winter.
He was walking through the snow with a bottle of Stalinskaya under
his arm.

Speech is a way of sneaking through
(subliminal)   *information,*
to help the ones who don't understand
(subliminally)
to understand   (what you want (subliminally)
to get it).

We have to be uniform. Dammit!

He slips on ice and falls on his behind.
Some kids start throwing hard snowballs toward him.

Part I:

Birds and beasts. Celebrity seizures

Preliminary issues

In time, several thinkers expressed opinions regarding the birds and beasts surrounding us, beings so common, yet always strangers to us.

1ˢᵗ Strophe: Gherea considered that a mammal doesn't exist in the concrete reality, as the horse, the elephant, the ox, the goat, or the dog exist. "Mammal" is just a generic name, necessary to the thought. Let's imagine now: a certain X would say that the mammal exists in the concrete, the same concrete way as the ox or the elephant; this of course would be an illusion, a Spuk. But there is also the reverse situation, in which another X would prove that the existence of the mammal is an illusion, and the horse, the ox, the elephant, being mammals, are an illusion as well.

1ˢᵗ Antistrophe: Often, language creates such confusions.

2ⁿᵈ Strophe: The ones who still remember Otto Weininger know that "people who created language faced similar impressions." Meaning, a number of words can modify, gradually or suddenly, the object they name.

2ⁿᵈ Antistrophe: The object disappears and instead, another one appears. Gradually or suddenly, the world (trans)forms.

3ʳᵈ Strophe: Change before the change/change that stops the change right at the starting point. Words like: "pigs," "camels," "monkeys," "oxen," "donkeys," or "dogs" now mean people, not at all animals. There is, in consequence, "a recognition of the fact that certain people embody certain animal possibilities. [...] The people inclined toward immorality get these traits as they grow old; more and more, they cede to those inclinations."

3rd Antistrophe: Gradually or suddenly, the animal disappears. Everywhere and forever, only the human.

Epode: "Unlike the animals, language doesn't assign/(gradually or suddenly) any character trait to the plants."

The bird, or about flying. The first seizure

1. Introduction
Birds are made of innocent but half-witted men who showed interest in heavenly matters, but who believed, in their simple-mindedness, that the surest evidence regarding those matters can be obtained with their own eyes. Those men grow feathers instead of hair.

2. Etymologies
They are called birds because they don't follow established paths, but move in indeterminate directions. They are winged because they aim to the heights with their wings and rise, rowing with them.

3. The Albatross
According to Heidegger: The questions arise from the dispute with the things. And the things exist only where there are eyes to see them. That said, he started to slowly grow bald until, without being indifferent to what was happening, he found that there was

nothing

left on his head. And, because Nothing wanted to remain, the Dasein grew there, out of nowhere, a few feathers, a welcome sight.

Finally, he thought he could fly. But

when he opened his wings, two giant eyes,
petrified with amazement, rolled on the asphalt. And no one
dared to look at them.   He became an albatross.

1ˢᵗ Strophe: They say *albatross* is the common name of over 23 species of birds from the *Diomedeidae* family. They vary in size from that of a goose to a swan.

(it's a well-known fact that Heidegger reached the largest dimensions of this species)

Albatrosses are widespread, from the Arctic to the tropics.

(and he liked extreme cold)

Sometimes, these birds spend months at sea, as they can sleep on the waves.

(The *Dasein* spent a lot of time there)

Plus, they are excellent predators

(of an uncommon voracity). They feed either on the young of other animals, or on marine birds.

1ˢᵗ Antistrophe: And in his simple-mindedness, Heidegger thought himself a Nazi. And in our simple-mindedness, we took him at his word.

2ⁿᵈ Strophe: Because the logos as "speech" *brings into sight (a sonorous expression through which something is brought into the field of vision each time)*

> but there are also basis, reason, judgment, concept, definition, relation

Finally, what was seen was only Death, a concept perfectly defined by reason beyond judgment on the basis of the relationship between humans and beasts (different species *divided into flocks, each one with its own leader who guarded them with the purpose of devouring them;*

let's not forget, România has a tradition of grazing). Now, there is only *logos*. We can see that clearly

with our own eyes, because we were given the eyes to obtain evidence in logical speech.

Death. Monarch. Beast. Famine. The need to eat out of the other (even when we're not hungry). Pleasure.

2nd Antistrophe: Stalin understood this the best, only he *didn't concern himself with philosophy and heavenly matters.* Unfortunately!

3rd Strophe: Speech is all we have left while we wait for our wings to grow. This way, we'll return to being birds!

3rd Antistrophe: But language lacks precisely this text. Unfortunately!

Epode: Flight is not a condition of innocence, maybe/only the feathers (but numerous exceptions still exist).

Impression from Olympus

Heavy sky. Weighing. On us,
oppressive. Dry wave
of time steps out from us, onto us.

Blue. Blue. Blue

gull that splinters. Cry
blue blue white
star. White moon seen through daylight.

1ˢᵗ Disambiguation

The difference between an albatross and a beast is best established by the EXD[1]:

ALBATROSS, *albatrosses,* noun, masculine. Marine flying bird similar to the tern but a lot larger, with white feathers and long, narrow, black-tipped wings (*Diomedea exulans*);

ALBATROSS, *albatrosses,* noun, masculine. The largest marine bird living in the Southern hemisphere, with wide wings, thick, curved beak, very greedy; it's one of the fast-flying birds, looking like a giant sea gull.

BEAST, *beasts,* noun, feminine. Large wild animal; brute. ♦ Fig. Person who is extremely mean, cruel, violent.

BEAST (Latin *fera*) s. f. **1.** Large wild animal; monster, savage. ♦ Fig. Person who is mean, cruel. **2.** (In the "Apocalypse") The personification of the Antichrist who will appear before the Second Coming of Christ: *the first beast* rises out of the sea, inciting the world peoples to war with the Church; *the second beast* (the dragon) rises out of the earth and is the false prophet.

The explanation of any term used is essential to speech coherence.

Hence, regarding the albatross and the beast, only two common elements are found at the linguistic level: large (an adjective) and sea (a noun). They don't apply to all the definitions every time. Their common link is not stated, though, only implied: greed, hunger; as a concrete result, the idea present in both definitions is cruelty.

---

[1]EXD=The explanatory dictionary of the Romanian language. As the reader noticed, we always return to this amazing book in which everything is ordered and registered in great detail.

Despite this, the albatross can fly. This would have been the difference between the two terms, if the Biblical beast wouldn't be often portrayed with wings (although without feathers; instead, scales are drawn).

2ⁿᵈ Disambiguation

The confusions appeared again when one strayed from these definitions. The word albatross, synonym with terms such as: poet, penitence, etc., was used in literature (see: Coleridge, Melville, Baudelaire, Mary Shelley etc.), described mostly as a bird,

flying toward empty azure skies where it could never breathe the air of absolute freedom. Because nothing is falser than freedom itself and the image of this bird, crossing

the heights.

In our society, the confusions follow a gradual adaptation to the free market economy:

1. Albatross: the name of a band that was famous years ago, playing at important life events:

http://www.trilulilu.ro/muzica-diverse/colaj-albatross-melodii-foarte-vechi-selectii
https://www.youtube.com/watch?v=sF9NLRhoGwE

2. The Albatross Resort, located at 4 km from Călărași, somewhere on the Borcea shore:

> **The Albatross Resort** *gets its special meaning in a place far from the city bustle, cooled by the shade of generous vegetation. It's an ideal spot for tourists who prefer resting, relaxation, and vacationing in a picturesque space, as well as the ones in transit to other destinations. The resort boasts a total number of 75 rooms, of which 33 singles with a double bed, 19 doubles, and 23 suites. The motel offers elegant, luxurious, and comfortable rooms with optimum conditions for resting in a select atmosphere. Included are*

amenities and services such as: AC, telephone, cable TV, minibar, ensuite bathroom (tub + shower), hair dryer, wireless and cable internet, safe for valuables, parking, breakfast included in the room price (Swedish buffet), room service.

The beast, or about hunger. The second seizure

1. Introduction

Terrestrial wild animals evolved from the ones that didn't bother with philosophy and heavenly matters because they couldn't use the revolutions as they pleased, letting themselves guided by those parts of the soul that reside in the chest.

2. Etymologies

The beast is in a permanent union with the dream world. There are no dreams without beasts,

and no beasts without dreams. They (re)produce each other despite the fact the beast has its head on its shoulders, and yet it's generated by an acephalous,

the dreamer. According to Isidor de Sevilla, *the name bestia is suitable for, literally, lions, cheetahs, tigers, wolves, foxes, as well as dogs, monkeys, and other animals that attack either with fangs, or with claws.*

They are called beasts, bestiae, *from dream, force, because they are violent.*

Here and now, the dream invades the animal head, the only place where it can find refuge, after wandering aimlessly through the acephalous, still body. Then again, Isidor de Sevilla: *they are called feral,* ferae, *because they are naturally free and let themselves wander,* ferantur, *as they please.* That's why the dream loves them so much. The dream and its need of free will

to kill, to eat.

3. The wolf

Sometimes,

According to Plutarch, some   animals

use reason, even an excess of it,   we could

                                               add.

1ˢᵗ Strophe: In the case of the old wolf, the excess of reasoning is a danger that threatens its species already almost extinct. But the dream nests inside its head and makes it much more tenacious. Plus, as Buffon teaches us, *the wolf is one of the animals most desirous of meat and, although it naturally has the necessary means to satisfy this desire and that it was, in a word, bestowed with everything it needs to find, attack, vanquish, catch, and devour its prey, it often almost dies of hunger. The wolf is by nature unrefined and cowardly, but, when in need, it becomes ingenious and daring.* Still, its reason, by overcoming the limits of any excessive rationale, stops it from reacting logically to its environment, the forest landscape, or the traditional village.

1ˢᵗ Antistrophe: *The wolf, raised from a pup, becomes tamed, but never attaches itself, because its wild nature is stronger than education.*

2ⁿᵈ Strophe: Often, you can see them in the middle of the night, under the yellow light of the moon, waiting for their big transformation, howling. Dream! Their fur falls, the fangs retract, and in propitious places/in a fertile matter, they bloom human hands

and feet.

[Because "night was given for the man to think what he will do during the day."]

The moment of maximum vulnerability. / The moment when it can be killed. / The moment favorable to the hunter.

2ⁿᵈ Antistrophe: The uneducated, the rude, the unacceptable, the inhuman. Derrida: *cruelty, criminality, law-less-ness, to not have faith and law,*

these are the characteristics of a wolf! For them, it deserves its fate.

Do not have mercy for the lone wolf. Kill it!

3rd Strophe: "The only real reform is the awakening of the humankind from the dream about itself." Marx's words were best understood by Stalin. He, with the help of Hitler

(a strange wolf subspecies that had wings, beak, and albatross claws)

engineered the big awakening. Instead of the head, they targeted the chest. That's where the breath, the voice resides. Let's (re)place the dream with the voice, that's the new dream! The birth of the word. And the beast will die, killed by a beast. *Homo homini lupus*, the one Rousseau didn't agree with. But, *the ferocity of the man towards his neighbor surpasses anything the animals can do, and, faced with the menace it presents to nature, even the carnivorous animals retreat from it, terrified. This cruelty itself implies being human. It dreams a neighbor, even a being from another species.* And to think, dear Mr. Lacan, that the wolf is a *hateful animal, with a despicable, wild appearance, with a terrifying howl, a foul smell, a dishonest nature, and ferocious habits,*

3rd Antistrophe: *a bad animal, harmful when alive and useless after death, save for its worthless fur*

4th Strophe: Lycanthropy is nothing but a mental disorder. *The imbecilic man and the animal are beings whose acts and results are the same in every respect, because one has no soul and the other doesn't use it in any way; both lack the power of reflection and in consequence they don't have understanding, nor brains, nor memory, but both have sensations, feeling, and movement.*

4th Antistrophe: Hitler and Stalin showed us! Now we know.

5th Strophe: The man-wolf, in the case of Sergei Pankeiev, who was seduced as a child by his sister only two years older than him, is a typical example of a stubborn wolf, for which the awakening functioned only sporadically, at specific times. The big hoax was in Sergei's stupidity, used as a weapon against the famous psychoanalyst, thus proving, at the same time, to Stalin and to Hitler, the reason of their failed mission. Stupidity, that's the dream!

Sergei was speaking, while the man-wolf didn't know how to speak. Sergei died, while the man-wolf is immortal. Sergei was a normal man like any other, while the man-wolf was a normal wolf like any other.

5th Antistrophe: In order to kill the beast, teach it to speak! That's when the great awakening occurs.

A trace of dream is always left outside the dream./A trace of silence is always left in language./A trace of stupidity is always left in stupidity.

6th Strophe: *Derrida, the same as al(ways): And the poem, if such a thing exists, and the thought, if such a thing exists, are related exactly to this im-probability of the breath. The breath remains, though, for some living things, at least, not only the first but also the last sign of life, of living life, the life that lives, that is alive. The first and last sign of living life.*

6th Antistrophe: The reason [*Here live the men and dogs. Other animals: hyenas, etc. Birds: the owls. No plants, no minerals. Draw your own conclusions. But all of them live according to the free zone, the men-dogs at the bottom. Here, history is made. Here, love is made. Everything, consciously. Here are the mean ones and the intelligent ones.*] of the excessive animal: Be stupid! Destroy the language! Destroy it! Everything that overflows is dirty. The liquid, be it red or without color, visible or resounding, is the carrier of these words we sentence to death. Spay it!

Epode: Finally, as trace, the last breath./ The sigh of the soul. The oh.[1] The beast, returned to the beast.

[1] Kittler:"Certainly, feeling and soul are also only translations, a nominalizing paraphrase of the sigh « oh! », as the unique signifier that is not a signifier."

The cattle, or about work.
The third seizure

1. Introduction

Shortly before becoming an albatross, Heidegger said that not only the animal doesn't have language, but it also doesn't work.

Regretfully, the existence of oxen complicates his demonstration.

2. Etymologies

From an etymological point of view, new horizons are envisioned. The clear establishment of the roles of the animals in human society:

We call cattle, pecus, any being without language and human face.

(back to the absence of language, cattle are the ones who don't speak their names) The sin of being an animal, to dare not to know your place, the answer to the question: Who are you?

Brand the cattle so they don't run astray! And that's how my signature on your body was born!

But *literally, the name animals, pecora, is used for those beings destined for food, such as sheep and pigs, or to those useful to human needs, like horses and oxen.* Work and food, food, and work. Work! Work and eat! We work and we eat/you eat! etc.

There is a difference between pecora, cattle, and pecudes, animals grown for their meat: because the ancient people gave all animals the name of pecora, but they called pecudes only the edible ones, edere, as in pecuedes. We always have to make this distinction:
the body-work/pecora and the body-food/pecudes. The two are different in roundness, tenderness, and color.

3. The ox

The ox, if we consider Buffon's writings, is among the animals most useful to the man; it secures the daily food

Spiritually, his image appears in prophecies: Ezekiel and his winged cart with four faces, the left one being an ox

In addition, the ox has the advantage of consuming very little. Without this animal, life would be hard!

The body—an image indicative of the work that someone can do in and for society, in and for its prosperity, yours and of the others. The ox is the one that accomplishes, in the end, everything. Silently, without being heard, because he is built that way. Only for this, the ox has been created:

The one who doesn't have an ox should buy one!

1ˢᵗ Strophe: *Its neck thickness and the breadth of its shoulders show the ox is most suitable for traction, but for that it needs to wear a yoke. Because of that— for the best traction—the yoke is especially designed to be placed onto the neck. It's strange that this way of yoking is not widely used and there are entire provinces where the ox is forced to pull with its horns. The only argument in favor of this practice is that, when the ox is harnessed by its horns, it's easier*

to drive.

"But you, the son of man, listen to me! Do not be stubborn! Open your mouth and eat everything I'm giving you!"

1ˢᵗ Antistrophe: Yoking is an extremely simple and profitable practice. It can be applied to other animals, especially horned ones; the ones without head outgrowth will be harnessed by the neck, often with additional devices which will make their neck thicker (when their body doesn't allow otherwise). In case of inefficient yoking, when the body doesn't show enough tenderness and freshness to be used as food, those animals will be chased away from the community into a hole dug for those species, right outside, around the area where the community is located. There, they can be fed, if anyone is willing

to do so.

2nd Strophe: One must consider the fact that the ox didn't exist in the first paradise where animals were provided for and where they didn't have to work, living with the sole purpose of entertaining their owners. In that place, a hunt was organized a few times per year in the auspicious periods. Outside of that, the animals were caught from time to time and brought before the curious viewers of all ages. Very few got to the dissection table,

for medical purposes.

2nd Antistrophe: What a noble end to be on such a table, in the name of the good, a death completely dedicated to the other! That was the dream of all the animals in

paradise.

3rd Strophe: Unfortunately, only a few were chosen. They say that, later, the ox appeared exactly from these species sacrificed on the science altar. Probably, a successful

experiment.

Who knows? In the beginning, a small number. Then, a herd, last I heard, without traces of hooves of the herd, because of too many traces erase unheard.

3rd Antistrophe: The herd, or the flock, as terms that name larger animal groups, have several disadvantages. First, they reference sheep and secondly, they include other domestic animals, eventually some wild ones. But they can bring to mind a crowd, or a group of people that must be in disarray, vagrant. From here, in an absolutely unprecedented way, comes the definition of a flock of believers. We have to mention, before closing this subject regarding this word, that the flock is directly related in language to the verb "to multiply" and the noun "multiplication". The last one attracts a series of strange consequences,

of which Buffon speaks:

4th Strophe: In the species used for flocks *where reproduction is very important, the female is more necessary and more useful than the male.* She produces

a fetus.

4th Antistrophe: and the fetus is the good *that grows and always renews itself. Its meat is a food that is plentiful, as well as healthy*

and tasty.

Epode: *Lots of families are forced to live daily/taking advantage of the cow on their farm!*

The man, or about manhood. Let's give the animal what is the animal's

1. Introduction

Derrida: *Sexuality in itself is often considered beastly; the sexual desire is the beast within, the most wild and greedy beast, and the most voracious one.*

Buffon: *As man is not a simple animal, and as his nature is superior to the one of the animals, we have to demonstrate the cause of this superiority and establish,*

with clear and solid proofs,

the exact degree of the inferiority of the animal's nature, in order to distinguish what only belongs to the man from what he has in common with the animal.

Heidegger (just before taking flight as an albatross): *The man has nothing in common with the animal.*

Latour: *In the world in which we live, however, humans and non-humans cannot be had separately. Our reality is a web of relations between human and non-human entities that form ever new realities on the basis of ever new connections.*

Where did we leave the animal?

2. The anatomy lesson

a) A few words about the penis and the seminal liquid. Theoretical concepts

The male reproductive system is not as complex as the female one. Its inferiority emphasizes once again its superiority: less developed, less animal-like. The female, through its anatomy, is a tamed beast.

In the following pages, we will describe this natural wonder through which nature denies its own nature,

I am all that exists, existed, and will exist, and no mortal ever lifted my veil!

the sublime, or the male reproductive system.

Structure: two testicles, the seminal vesicles, the Cowper glands, the vas deferens, the ejaculatory ducts, the epididymis, the prostate, the urethra, the scrotum and

the Penis.

The role of this system is to produce the sperm and to eject it to the exterior, through the Penis, as a jet, a process called ejaculation.

Herman Melville: *the jet is nothing but fog.*

I am drawn to this conclusion, besides other reasons, by my reflections about the grandeur and the sublime character of the Penis. I am not considering it at all as a regular being, superficial, because it is never found [...] as other similar species are found.

The Penis is both level-headed and profound. And I am convinced that, from all the heads of level-headed and profound people, such as Platon, Pyrrhus, The Devil, Jupiter, Dante, etc,. a half-visible vapor always rises in the moments they are deep in thought. One day, as I was working on a small treaty about Eternity, I had the curiosity to look at myself in a mirror, and, soon enough, I saw the reflection of a strange spiral unwinding in the air above my head.

So, the connection between the head and the Penis is established by the possibility of the ejaculation of a whitish substance of variable shape and consistency, but with the same function,

Reproduction.

Scientifically: Everything was rigorously demonstrated by Lacan, the one who discovered the presence of the Penis at the center of language.

The Penis or the copulative

organ is a body part (often belonging to the male sex) that is short, cylindrical, and mobile, suspended in the front of the pubic arch. It is made of three masses of cavernous tissue, wrapped in a fibrous sheath, covered at the exterior by skin. The two lateral masses are known as the corpora cavernosa, and the central one as *corpus spongiosum*. The last one contains the urethra. They form the erectile tissue, because the spongy spaces fill with blood when excited, and the penis becomes

rigid. Erection is the first consequence of the male sexual stimulation.

The Penis ends with the glans where the urethra opens to the exterior. *Its tegument, of a darker color, is an extension of the abdominal one; at the point where it meets the glans, it folds back to form a cutaneous sleeve, ending in a cul- de-sac, the foreskin. During an erection, the foreskin can retract partially or totally behind the glans, leaving it exposed to physical excitation,*

but also to accidents and irritations. Protect it! The nations that don't protect their foreskin and don't defend their Penis are a menace and must be eliminated.

Everything is about anatomy.

Unfortunately, the study of the copulative organ was only recently possible. Initially, it was thought irrecoverable when Isis, after killing Osiris, found all the fragments of his body except this essential one. Some even believed it didn't exist. But for us, the mystery was solved. The Penis was found.

Let's dissect and analyze it!

b) The dissection

The dissection is performed usually on a lifeless body after it spent a considerably long time in a special liquid, a solution of water and formaldehyde called formol, a very strong disinfectant and antiseptic. By using formol, the body becomes a secure, clean, and preserved medium ready for a safe examination.

Necessary materials: scalpel, scissors, two tweezers, surgical gloves, a Penis of acceptable dimensions.

[**Did you know that ...** Whales and elephants have the most impressive organs (both in length and in circumference) from the animal kingdom. Scientists have established that whales have the largest Penis in the world, and not the elephants. On average, the whale Penis is up to 3 meters long, its exact dimension being hard to determine, as it would need to be measured during mating.]

Once the above materials are gathered, one could start by opening the organ with the purpose of studying its anatomy. One would try to reveal, as best possible, all the parts presented in section a). At the end, the one who performed the dissection will invite the audience to ask questions related to the less-clear moments of the procedure.

c) Uses of the information resulted from the research

Finally, no trace will be left,
as if the trace could exist as a clue;
in the end, no sign is traced without trace.

＊

Commercial break/Turned time:

Behold the car of your dreams: *Dartz Prombron Monaco Red Diamond Edition,*

a Russian replica

of the more well-known Hummer, the most expensive SUV in the world, sold for $1,450,000. With windows plated in gold foil, exhaust pipe made of pure tungsten, and diamonds-studded dashboard, the car comes equipped with three of the most expensive Vodka in the world, the "Russo-Baltique Vodka" sold in 2008 for 790,000 British pounds.

In addition, the leather upholstery is made of whale Penis.

The model Dartz Prombron Monaco weighs four tons, has an engine of 450 horsepower, and can withstand a missile attack

due to its Kevlar armor, the same compound material used for anti-bullet vests.

Buy the Dartz Prombron Monaco Red Diamond Edition! Drive fearless, sitting on the largest penis in the world!

Buy! Drive! Be!

3. Ravenously hungry. An event

All week, he fucked only whores he picked up on the road.
Now, he was holding in his hands the last money he had from his
    grandma,
        Thinking to get something to eat
        or another woman.

Then, he found himself in front of her   not in the mood.
He found himself in this room   tired and hungry.
    I just want to watch you, go ahead and undress.
    No, better yet, take off your panties and stand there.

He felt his stomach grinding   mercilessly.
Instead of feeding him,   it was biting his body
        on the inside.
    I can't stay with you all night.
    You have to finish faster.

The whore's voice was melodious   and young,
Extremely young, no more than   16 years old
    Her thin thighs, uncovered by the butt-long skirt.
    (*What the hell is a child doing in my apartment?*)

He only wanted to see here, where she used to   live. Why isn't
        he getting it?
He gave her all the money   for this.
    His stomach shrunk strongly, cutting off his breath.
    I can't stay with you all night. You've paid me way too little.

Her lazy voice became increasingly pleading. *Please, please!*
He just watched her in silence   fixated, without moving.
        She sobbed.

Why is she continuing her moron cry?
It's devouring me alive. Don't you feel it, bitch!?

In the dark, he touched her thigh. Soft   and thin. But still
                                                      she didn't
                                                      stop.

Each sigh, a punch in his stomach. He held her   with his last
                                                      strength.

          It seems she quieted a little. It seems
          his pain quieted, too.

Suddenly, he woke up. He had his penis   deeply thrusted into
                                                      her anus.

Tears were dripping on his hand, or maybe   sweat. It didn't
                                                      matter.

          The biting of the stomach died down.
          The sounds stopped. The pain was gone.

I can't pay you for this, call whomever you want. I don't care!
He got off her   and his stomach started to bite his body again.
          Let me go. I have to go.
          I can't stay with you all night.

Leave! To hell with you, bitch! He opened the door   wide, pushing her
                                                      out.

Why can't she feel that I am eaten alive?   *Why can't she?*
          His shadow overlapped hers.
          A ray of light touched their faces.

For the first time, they looked at each other. Their faces were thin and pale.
Their bodies were sobbing.

Somewhere deep inside each one, an odious stomach was biting mercilessly
from their flesh.

Part II:

The phallic phase

What do you say now, mister Plato?

Osiris' penis was found and dis/sected; together, let's restore the woman's phallic dignity!

1. Introduction

This is what we'll continue to state: the ones who were born men but who were cowards and lived their life badly will be reborn later, according to the credible myth, as women[1].

[**Did you know that ...** Some solved the problem of the manhood and the two sexes much more elegantly, without Platon's help: the Aztecs believed the women who died in labor were going to the same place as the sacrificed warriors or the fighters fallen in battle. The women replaced the warriors at noon, joining the sun on its second half of the journey in the day sky.]

Let's treat the errors of nature!

---

[1]In consequence, Plato considers the woman doesn't even exist; everything is a matter between men. In other words, it's between manly men and men without manhood, the cowards. The woman is the man with a manhood error. A big discrepancy occurs at the moment of the important discovery of the Y chromosome, originated from an X chromosome. From a genetical point of view, only women exist: women without and with a Penis. The man is a woman as a genetic error. Besides these errors, the human race is haunted by even more discrepancies. Exemplary is the case of Rousseau and his strange disease in which the natural balance between the excretory and the reproductory functions of the penis is disrupted in favor of the first. In time, the disease will cause the almost total loss of Rousseau's manhood, so he will become a woman. Although, scientifically speaking, the disease will help correct the genetic error of having the Y chromosome, *the catastrophic perversion* brought him health.

2. Therapy

They cleaved the head into two because it was too big. And the head became

small, really small,

and glued itself back.

Nothing　　　　Never　　　　Ever　　　　Without　　　　Head!

The body (short movie in four frames)

What exists is a sexual body.

Frame 1

On its surface (an uneven, steep, and toxic space), infinite populations lived.

Frame 2

Mars embracing Venus in a sleep with no return. They turn; their hate ends in a mating dream, the father penetrating his daughter's vagina while she greedily licks the maternal clit– ménage à trois; she can bite them, the moment she was long waiting for is here, she's feasting on her parents, enthusiastically chewing the paternal penis and her mother's vulva, she sucks their blood and rips skin strips, exposing the interior of a world from which they always hid. She swallowed them.

Frame 3

Naked women bodies. Almost dry   one after the other   and bones that pierce the skin. The air was almost exploding under the weight of the commands. No one can understand anything else. The only form of communication resounded harshly into the ears of the ones waiting. From time to time, a vagina would open like a cactus flower. A sudden move of acceptance. Each one of them was swimming through the sea of bodies without thinking about their way. Where to? Only a rustle of weak arms. The words crowded faster and faster   more and more. Not a drop of silence in the deep silence. Often, the night blizzard buries everything under the leaves.

Frame 4

The space as *matter's fundamental shape of existence, inseparable from it, with the appearance of an uninterrupted whole with three dimensions, and which expresses the order of the objects and processes*, can be filled. And it was. The objects suffocated their surroundings. They always arrived in successive waves, continuously, brought by the South wind. Countless. Round breasts, full like blooming hills, smooth thighs, arms whiter than the memory of snow, and … maybe, the lips, the plump woman's lips that started to ripen. He tasted this fruit, delicious and tender, crushed in his teeth:

For efficient sex, follow Figure I./ The order of the positions must not change./ Nothing more, nothing less, maybe just a gesture,/ like a syllable that sneaked into the words.

The hands are never apart/ From the body that will be penetrated, and the opening/ of the legs is calculated depending on/ the degree of bending and the curvature of the spine.

The penis penetrates the vulva after reaching/ One of the dimensions indicated in/ the Figure. One should not forget finding the proper and necessary level/ of wetness of the vulva.

Following the above instructions ensures/an efficient orgasm 90% of the times./ The remaining 10% is in the gesture si-/ milar to the sound found in the mo-/ notonous running of a fix number of sylla-/ bles.

The main character featured in the frames:

In the beginning: there was only a face.

A white screen and a few dots

I
N
V
I
S
I
B
L
E
Then, the figure 1
111111111111111111111111111111111111111111111111111111111111111111111111111111111111
A single row,
W
I
T
H
O
U
T
words,
w
i
t
h
o
u
t
letters

In the end: THE END
And lastly, the last trace.

The imagined monologue, attached to the frames:

wretch! whore cunt slut rag bitch scrubber slapper slag harlot trollop
dishrag wanton doxy drab quean trull wench scrap slattern shred flop
cocotte tart madame pro moll brass nail tom strumpet floozie scoundrel
hooker ho roundheel slut whore hustler pussy puta pudenda beaver
twat snatch rag stink stench baggage defiled gash monkey foul hag cad
boorwoman tramp slut bitch

Background sound:

With two straws and with two threads / Who's the one that moonlight
bends/ Burning coal and burning fire/ half her ugly body's pyre?

With two threads and with two straws / Who's the one who dying
knows /How to rise from underground/ A red dance unseen, unbound?

The collectivization of the voice

1st Strophe: May my name be România/the one of all who threw their phallus to the dogs, glory to you women non-women you, the ones who can't bear children in your wombs! Glory to you in the name of our father who, by tearing out his organ, he gifted you so you can drink; she, born out of his penis, not from his thigh like all of us; she, born from the self-sacrifice of the son in the name of the father, his woman, unlike all the others, has something immoral and perverse in gestures in words has the nerve to show us precisely the most dreadful traits that anyone else but her would try hiding them

1st Antistrophe: "The woman is not human. The more so as women, in fact, don't think. They mimic human thinking. As with the aliens in the horror-SF movies, they borrow rapidly from their surroundings, expressions, phrases, entire ready-made thoughts that they assemble and deliver lively, without the slightest psychic adhesion to what they are saying."

2nd Strophe: May my name be România/her soles, heavy with mud, pressing on the clean asphalt, then the stains that cannot be wiped clean, the heaviness of the dissimulations, who are you? Forever equal in their differences, a body grown over death's brink, alive, it brings life, it carries it everywhere, it gives birth to it in the place where they killed, a place suffocated by white bodies, at the wake of the ones remaining, teeming with hired mourners announcing the resurrection pain

2nd Antistrophe: "The heaviest task in a marriage is the man's; without hesitation, he has to support, to be his wife's shield, in any circumstance, forever. If we'd had to admit that she is his equal, we'd have to demand the same of her. We don't, and she still revolts. [...] She, in the hours of holy spell, would like to be a man—wishing to reap all the sensations of the universe, to be everything. [...] But everything is limited to an imitation more or less perfect; the power of inventivity, the creative spirit won't be found in a woman."

3ʳᵈ Strophe: May my name be România/and you will flood the world, the hands busy with guns, the mouths full of desire without need without pain the impetuous whirlpool of revolt is where you'll lay your newborns, the men killed next to your sacrificed breast, and your arm will fulfill your chaste body from now on, and your remaining breast will satiate the hunger of the woods where the wolves will blossom like a crazy spring

3ʳᵈ Antistrophe: "After birth, the baby will suckle on the breast very often, so you will have to dedicate almost all your time to this activity, as well as to eat and rest. No need to do that major cleaning that can be postponed for now. This indestructible bond between you and your baby can only happen once. Keep some food and water close by, because you'll spend a lot of time breastfeeding. You will want to go out sometimes, but at least two weeks have to pass before you'll have a long-enough time, 2-3 hours between feedings, so you can take the baby for a walk during that time."

4ᵗʰ Strophe: May my name be România/where the mountains give shelter to terrible palaces, and people-animals with sharp teeth whose belly longs for blood, nothing will quench a thirst like theirs, the young body of the she-wolf forever hidden from light, untouched by the sun, lights up its own sunrays in unrivaled ecstasy, whiplashed, it feels voluptuous pleasures, and the chains that bind it in its casket fall each night at that late hour the Transmittance Law takes effect
Contamination: *you have to bite, to suck someone's blood, to strike terror in order to save this* principle! Eternal reproduction of the same being, who are you?

4ᵗʰ Antistrophe: "The one who is loved like a mother, loved and respected like a wife and has many more privileges... it's not right that she becomes a revolutionary, an anarchist. A young girl raised in such principles, in the poisonous fumes of discontent, what purpose could she have in the Society? [...] From such mothers, what kind of children would shape up, what education could be imposed following such morality? [...] The woman, by using the culture obtained from schools, in her family, by developing the home-making industries, by creating a cult from raising and educating her children, by being their first doctor, and their first soul counselor, will significantly lighten the state burden, giving it well-shaped people, supportive elements, not ones that require support."

Epode: "We will vigorously protest against the tendencies of those who will create obstacles to progress through the utopia of their pretentions. [...] This aspect will not be raised here, the Romanian women cannot be agitated, because... that would destroy the peace of the state. The energies consumed in this direction, if channeled towards other goals, would achieve a much greater benefit of the culture and national progress. We have to uplift morality.

In our country, the cultural emancipation of the men must be imposed, [...] but never *The Absolute Emancipation of the Woman*." Let our name be România!

The perforated space

But once, in the abyss,
lucid ghosts trembled under the days' decomposed fog.
No gesture could pierce their viscous placenta.

In the absence of the skeleton,
the skin of the dead emerged, crawled from the urns along the twilight.
No gesture could stop their sliding into the waves.

One over the other,
rotten, mixing through rough touches, white tissues, full of grass and
mud, without the hardness of the burnt bones, without vertebrae
thrust into the powder, snaking toward the top on a dry mountain,
among parched boulders and brambles, leafless bushes that rustle
with every whimper.

One over the other,
the remains of the bodies, thin strips of dehydrated flesh moved in the
sticky, humid air like a yellowish paste, stolen by the wind, dragged through
the other's ashes, restless, without the night in which we often touch our
organs to reassure ourselves of their presence and of our own life.

> And only in those evenings of love and cold,
> *our experience proves that the matters we think are dead,*
> *the rotten matters, always moved from the outside,*
> *regain their activity and life when combined in certain ways.*
>
> The woman, a collection of holes dug into skin,
> is breathless since a long time.
> your hand will glide over the hills of her body,
> your hand will bleed over her shapeless breasts,
> without a sigh, without a gesture in response.

It's true, to cover the cities and stones with green,
thick roots would have to sink deep into darkness,
and the clean skeleton would rise from the still-wet dust,
with soft knees, looking for the watery dirt,
the hard phalanges would thrust into it, silently,
and dig, wanting to be buried,
to build a daily shield from the mud.

The eyes, lifted from each cavernous hole,
bigger and bigger/more and more

Will search for light,
even more fiery/even more.

Black bodies, suffocated lungs, coal, gray days, split nails, torn
        clothes,
and night.

The metallurgic land: "To pierce the mountains instead of
climbing them/ To dig the earth instead of raking it/ To punch
the space instead of smoothing it

to transform the earth into Swiss cheese."

Get out!

Then your blood will strongly pulse in your veins,
rational spirits will frolic in the void between you,
free impulses will reign over the movement of the limbs.

Get out!

Now, no sigh, no movement,
only the stiff woman and the hand
that searches/bleeds/digs

on surfaces.

And you wait.

Part III:

Punch! And they bit

A modern and contemporary bio-ethic

1st Strophe: Following, we analyze the final product of the coupling of a woman with a man:
The child.
The child is
co-created by the two then the woman gives birth[1]. Maternity means when the woman's womb grows round gradually, for nine months, with a higher frequency in the last three months. After that, begins the process of delivery, which varies from a few hours to one or two days. Finally, a new individual appears who doesn't produce but only consumes for a certain period depending on the context.

1st Antistrophe: "The child, after it's born, is irrelevant from a moral point of view and doesn't have the right to live. Babies are potential persons and not real ones; they are not considered human beings until the moment their parents decide that. It's not possible to affect a newborn if you prevent it from developing its potential to become a person in a relevant sense from a moral point of view. The life of the baby starts when the parent decides."

2nd Strophe: What are children?

2nd Antistrophe: Child = boy or girl in the first years of life (until adolescence)

3rd Strophe: From a grammatical point of view, "the children" is a common noun, simple, definite articulated, plural.

3rd Antistrophe: Disambiguation one: child equals

---

[1]"By approaching human beings not only in terms of their being-in-the-world but also in terms of their coming-in-the-world, they not only appear as *subject* but also as *objects*, not only as the *res cogitans* of their consciousness but also as their *res extensa* of their bodies with which they experience and act in the world."

Offspring grown from the bottom of the plant's stem, from the fist node
Wooden or metal nail thrust into the hinge from the door or gate pole

4th Strophe: From a literary point of view, there are many confusions regarding this category of individuals; it's not possible to find clear elements that could be introduced in a correct argument.

4th Antistrophe: Second Disambiguation: child equals
    A naïve, inexperienced person

5th Strophe: From a social point of view, children are the consequences of he and she getting closer. Falling in love. The woman loves the man and the man loves the woman. This is clear—history has proven it. The state knows all these things and encourages the love between them. The more they love each other, the stronger the state grows. And happier. To show its gratitude, the State created the Family. Inside the family, they can legally love each other, in other words: invisible love becomes visible, materializing at the surface. But any framework has its boundaries. Thus, the children can appear within the framework or outside it. Regardless of where they come from, they are loved. The State creates a new framework for the children without one, so they are not left out.

5th Antistrophe: "The newborns don't have the right to live, and the parents can decide to kill their children from various reasons: if they feel they can't bear the costs of raising the child, if they realize they can't take care and educate him, if the baby cries a lot, if he's not good looking or doesn't have the eyes of a certain family member. The parents will decide if a child born alive is truly alive. They can choose if the baby should live or not because babies are not people."

6th Strophe: The child would be "a cheek, a round face, a round body, curled around a mouth and an anus ... Something that sucks and eliminates and again sucks and again eliminates ..."

6th Antistrophe: In fact, "there are no children, and the problem of the consciousness is not only a human problem. [...] This (consciousness) is a general state of the human that he has probably in the fetus phase ... A millennia-long disease that shows no signs of weakness ..."

Epode: The children are overcome with love from everywhere and always. Mama could eat them up!

The price of flesh

1. The ballad of the woman behind the counter (replay)

The ballad of the woman behind the counter is a ballad that speaks about a wooden, moldy counter and the woman who stands behind it.

The significance of the woman and the counter are not specified in the poem.

Look closely at the counter.
It's old, made of cherry wood of superior quality, they don't make them like this anymore,
only it's pierced by woodworms.

The scents wafting off the counter are the remains of all the products that rested there through history.

The link between the woman and the counter is the virginity lost by the former on the latter when the woman was only 14, with one of the regular clients.

Now, she uses it to give the goods and to rest her breasts on it, because the woman's breasts are the real deal. These giants hide under them the store treasure, the coins used to give change to the customers. The breasts are longish with large, dark brown nipples, but with the disadvantage of perspiring profusely, so the coins are always damp. Despite that, the clients are happy, smiling wide.

The ones who love these breasts the most are the children who bite and suckle them greedily.

She's crazy about them and shouts:
Let the children come to me!

2. The free market. March 27, 1947

County of Bălți Prosecutor's Office
Arrested the residents of Sângerei village:

Țurcan Afajia, Țurcan Daria, and Țurcan Eudochia.

They are accused that, on March 17, 1947,
They invited as a houseguest   citizen Chiriac Zinovia
And strangled   citizen Chiriac Zinovia

Part of   her flesh they used
For food, and part of   her flesh they sold
At the Bălți market,

Priced at 40 rubles per kilogram.

3. Meat

Meat is the best food. The doctors recommend it. Consumption of

Meat increases intelligence and helps the body develop harmoniously. The populations that don't use

Meat in their diet are backward from an intellectual point of view.

Meat is used in many weight loss regimens. Generally speaking, the sources of

Meat are: various animals, preferably domestic ones, rarely wild. The difference is in the taste, tenderness, but also in the quantity of

Meat resulted from carving. Protein deficiency can result in serious diseases, such as: breast cancer, colon cancer, low cardiac frequency, cardiovascular disease, anemia, etc.
The trifunctional protein deficiency (TFP) is a rare disease that appears in children as well as in adults. Lastly, even death can occur. That's all for now about

Meat.

4. "Everyone died" (in eight episodes and an ending)

Pilot episode: On the houses' doors, they wrote "Everyone died!"

When the action takes place: February 13, 1947

Protagonists:

> Deputy President of the People's Commissaries of the MSSR*[1], comrade N. Smorigo
> Chief Chancellor of the People's Commissaries of the MSSR, comrade L. Diacenko
> Prosecutor of the MSSR, State judicial counsellor, comrade Colesnic
> Attorney General of the USSR, comrade Gorsenin C.P.
> Peasants of both sexes, residents of various villages and districts
> Children

Plot: Decision nr.13, from January 6, 1945, regarding the wheat export to the Habarovsc and Primorsc regions, Decides:

1. To mandate the chief of the *lugozagotzerno* office, comrade Tevosean, to ship to the Habarovsc and Primorsc regions 40,000 tons of grains, including: 24,000 tons in January and 16,000 tons in February.

2. The chief of the Chişinău railroad, comrade Banivețki, must provide train cars to be loaded and shipped according to the *lugozagotzerno's* requests.

3. To mandate the presidents of the county and district committees to ensure completion of the transport plan of the bread to localities without access to train stations.

4. In charge with verifying compliance with this decision will be the State Inspection Commissariat of the MSSR.

---

[1]MSSR= Moldavian Soviet Socialist Republic

The climax: Special report "Concerning the hard situation of the population of the MSSR"

"Through the present report, I consider it is my duty to inform you of the following:
Because of the drought and the lack of crops, there were created extremely difficult conditions regarding the food situation which led to complications within the population, especially in villages, causing mass dystrophy, increase of mortality, and cases of cannibalism.

From the preliminary information, until February 5, 1947, in the Republic were reported 213,000 cases of dystrophy, of which children up to 4 years old: 39,000 cases; between 4 and 14 years old: 33,000 cases. 14,000 beds in temporary barracks were installed. In total, 9,000 people were deceased.

The number of sick and of deceased grows day by day. For example, from February 1 to February 5th, the number of dystrophy cases has grown with 24,000 people; in these five days, 2,000 people were deceased.

34 cases of cannibalism were discovered (the certificates with detailed descriptions are attached). On February 6, 1947, the Office of the CC of WCP* passed the resolution which mentions the rise in criminality regarding the food problem and recommends the measures taken to help the Ministry of Internal Affairs by the party and soviet authorities and even the population, to defend and intensify the fight against criminality.

These things I had to report."

Protagonists' voices/survivor testimonies collected by Alexei Vakulovski:

Voice 1: We were eating even weeds. We mixed them with milk, sprinkled them with a handful of bulgur, and ate them. Today we feed even the cattle better food, but then ... Then, in Purcari, some women ate two kids. The kids were without parents: their father was in prison, and their mother died of hunger. Those women called the kids over and ate them. Their heads and all their remains were found later. The women were taken to prison.

Voice 2: Only hunger shouldn't exist. Because hunger … hunger wouldn't have killed so many people if they hadn't taken all the bread from our homes.

Voice 3: Terrible things were happening. What could be more terrible than sacrificing children? A man from Palanca, or from Tudora, smelled burned meat near a house. He went in and saw someone who had lost his mind, pushing a child into the oven and getting ready to eat him. In our village, I don't think there were such cases, although the people bulged with hunger and died daily. Can you imagine a village where there isn't a rooster crowing? Strange, isn't it? That's how our Antoneşti village was during the hunger.

Voice 4: One time, mother made *mămăligă* and I put aside some of it for the boys, for Valentin and Gică, I only had them at the time, so they can eat when they are back from school at noon. But a Gypsy man came into the house, saw the *mămăligă* on the stove, reached out and took it. Mother blocked his way and said: "Don't take all of it, leave my boys a piece." That's what they did: they shared that piece of *mămăligă*. That man ate his piece, then got out of the house.

Voice 5: During the hunger, people didn't talk to each other. They looked at each other and went on their way if they didn't see in the other's hand something to eat.

Voice 6: They were buried without coffins; many times they put several bodies in a hole, in common graves. Two of my sister's children died then as well. They died of hunger. They were older, one was in school, I think. They didn't have a life, poor kids … That time, you didn't think of others. You were trying to safeguard your own life.

Voice 7: I heard that in some other towns the parents ate their own children, they say people ate other people only to live, to stay alive. When I was driving vegetables to the other side of the Dniester, some friends of mine, drivers, showed me a man and said: "Here, this one ate a man's flesh during hunger." I went closer to him and watched him carefully: he had savage eyes.

Voice 8: We stopped at a train station and I remember how uncle Luca comes closer, touches my shoulder, and says: "Foca, give me a piece of bread because I can't stand anymore." He was exhausted, he couldn't go any further. We left him there… When we got back, we didn't find him. No one knew anything of him. Old man Luca died there. I told you: who cared at that time for another? Who? Old man Luca's son was with us as well. Yes, and he left behind his own father. In fact, no one could save him. If you were weaker, or with mercy, you could die, too …

Voice 9: Yes, surely more people died during the hunger than during the war.

Voice 10: Everywhere you looked, you could see people on their porches dozing off like chicken. No one gave them food, they didn't have any grains, and they sat facing the sun until they closed their eyes. Walking on the road, you could see dead people. Lying there, until their relatives would hear and came to take them. In the beginning of the hunger, the village was full of sobs; later, no one was crying. They were burying the people in silence.

Episode 1

January 17, 1947, Cotovski district, Caracui village

There was a case of homicide and using for food of a two-year-old child. On January 18, 1947, citizen Şveţ Evdochia Sergheevna goes to get her bread ration where she spends an hour or two. Coming back home, she finds her daughter Vasiliţa, aged 2, dead. The girl's body was cut into two pieces. The murderers turn out to be the three other siblings: Serghei, 11 years old, Maria, 8 years old, and Vasile, 5 years old. The day before, Serghei suggested to his mother to kill Vasiliţa. The mother opposed categorically and forbade him to do this odious murder. But when she came back from the point of bread distribution, the three children have already eaten the body and the legs. Upon investigation, is found that the Şveţ family lives in unbelievable squalor. The woman's husband died 10 days ago, leaving her with four children. They are sick with grade 2 and 3 dystrophy; they have eaten cat and dog meat before.

They were isolated in a home for dystrophy patients.

Episode 2

January 22,1947, Mileşti village

Scarevnea Stepan Stepanovici, born in 1912, poor peasant, aiding and abetting his sister, Graur Anastasia Feodorovna, 48 years old, murdered the daughter of the latter, Parascovia, 3 years old, and ate her. After a few days, with the same purpose, Scarevnea killed his sister, Graur Anastasia Feodorovna. In the current month of January, Scarevnea brought to his house four teenagers' bodies, of which one he used for food, another one he gave to Scarevnea Vera Antonovna, and two bodies of girls, aged between 7 and 10 years old, he cut to pieces and brought to the Cigherleni village. In addition, at his house was found the body of a 14-year-old teenager without head, arms, and legs, hidden in the stove, covered with clothes. Scarevnea is physically healthy, has received often his food ration, which he partially sold.

He was arrested.

Episode 3

January 25, Tresteni village, Chișinău County

Caracuian Grigorii Andreevici, born in 1903, medium income peasant, cut his son, Iacob, born in 1933, and ate him together with the family.

Caracuian was arrested.

Episode 4

December 23, 1946, Taraclia village, Taraclia district

Citizen Randopula M.I., poor Bulgarian ethnic, gave birth to a child on December 21, 1946. On December 23, 1946, she kills the baby and eats him.

Randopula was arrested.

Episode 5

February 7, 1947, Baurci village, Congaz district

Citizen Ialanin Andrei Ivanovici, born in 1916, Orthodox Turk ethnic, in agreement with his wife, cuts up his own daughter, aged 6, and eats her.

Ialanin was arrested.

Episode 6

January 26, 1947, Besalia village

Citizen Ciacu Gheorghii Gheorghievici, born in 1912, poor peasant of Orthodox Turkish ethnicity, cuts up his daughter, born in 1940, and consumes her as food. On January 28, the same individual kills his son, aged 5. Some of the flesh he eats, and some he tries to sell to the market.

He was arrested.

Episode 7

January 23, 1947, Sadaclia village, Roman district

Cardarar Ioana, born in 1906, in complicity with her sister, killed her son aged six. They cut him to pieces that they boiled to be consumed as food. Cardarar is a Gypsy ethnic. She doesn't possess land or wealth.

She is a nomad.

Episode 8

December 24, 1946, 7 a.m., Grigoriopol district (on the left bank of the Dniester River), Sipca village

Bulat Aculina, born in 1910, not married, cuts to pieces, with an axe, her eight-year-old son, then she boils and eats him.

Bulat was arrested. She confessed the murder.

Ending:

"According to the order of the Internal Affairs Ministry of the MSSR,

All the accused of cannibalism will be escorted to Chişinău city, to prison nr. 2.

In many cases, the investigation is closed, but, because many defendants are sick with acute dystrophy, we can't possibly escort them to prison, which delays the judicial proceedings, in closed sessions, of the

Supreme Court of the MSSR."

Experiment, experiment!

1. A few marginal experiments

The year 1953,

1ˢᵗ Strophe: Researchers administered radioactive iodine to a cohort of newborns at only 36 hours from birth in order to measure the concentration of the substance in the thyroid glands of the babies.

1ˢᵗ Antistrophe: *The human embryos can be used for experiments even in the intra-uterine phase, as cellular division, metabolical activity, and hormonal evolution are influenced by various substances.*

> **Refrain:** "No document referring to experiments on humans, which could provoke adverse reactions in the public opinion or could lead to criminal investigations, can ever be made public."

2ⁿᵈ Strophe: Several pregnant women were administered radioactive iodine in order to study, on the embryos subsequently aborted, in what phase of exposure they were, as well as the quantities of the substance that passed through the placenta barrier.

2ⁿᵈ Antistrophe: *To propose the necessary means for improving the human race leads us to studying first the origin of evil, in other words, heredity.*

> **Refrain:** "No document referring to experiments on humans, which could provoke adverse reactions in the public opinion or could lead to criminal investigations, can ever be made public."

The year 1895,

3ʳᵈ Strophe: Two mentally retarded boys were infected with gonorrhea to observe its effects on children.

3rd Antistrophe: *All the parts born from developing the first ovular generating cells will be able to be modified for the better or for the worst.*

> **Refrain:** "No document referring to experiments on humans, which could provoke adverse reactions in the public opinion or could lead to criminal investigations, can ever be made public."

The year 2004,

4th Strophe: In exchange for the children selected for tests with chemical substances, each family was offered the fix sum of $970, a cheap video camera, a t-shirt with the company logo, and a diploma of appreciation.

4th Antistrophe: *A child resembles the parent not only/physically, but also morally and through their capabilities.*

Epode: Heredity is also social, in other words it can intervene in the evolution of the civilizations,
Through labor or through a hereditary occupation; and, due to this occupation,/The civilized peoples gain aptitudes and tastes that prevent them from returning/to barbarism and offer a solid base for developing even stronger aptitudes,
> More distinguished tastes
> Better inclinations.

The purest races, the least mixed ones, are less exposed to diseases.

Unfortunately, social heredity doesn't exist/ In many people, so we'll speak only/ About Europe we'll say the lack of it is evident/ among people of the Far East, and this/ I think it has/ as an essential base/ the lack of a perfect/ civilization on one / hand, and on/ the other hand, the climate,
> The earth, in many places,
> Ingrate, inhabited by easterners.

The purest races, the least mixed ones, are less exposed to diseases.

We can't have the same/ Vegetables, animals,
Perfect people/ as the continental areas.

No one is better positioned to know about the progressive decreasing of the human race as the doctor: he is in each moment in a relationship with all the classes of the society; in consequence only he

is given the study of the necessary means in order to take measures for improving the race, because he alone sees and appreciates at the same time the movement of the general population, considering the moral and physical state of each mortal.

2. Ars poetica

Language—the First Protest Against the Final Solution

the biggest problem they had/ was the lice.

But poetry has to be a beautiful representation,
poetry must conquer every day banality.

Then and only then,
the woman was cutting with an unsharpened razor.

Then and only then,
she was stepping over the piles of feces spread in the room.

But poetry has to talk only about me
poetry has to be chockful of originalityORiginAL.

Give them less to eat/ and they will shit less.

Language—the most vicious entity. "An absolutely normal
physiologic process."

But poetry must be ...

3. Room nr. 5

Once,

the severely handicapped children were sent to Cighid.

The home capacity was of 120 beds, but half of these children died each year. 137 children died there. The majority of the deceased were 3-years-old. The center was located in a former castle, successfully claimed later by the family of the Hungarian count Tisza.
It functioned between 1987 and 1989, plus a short while after the revolution.

*

Against any personal communication.
Against any hallucinating ego.
Only the cold analysis of the images between us.

*

In the Romanian system, they were called "irrecoverable."

"These kids should have been killed immediately after birth." "Did it happen that you grew attached of any child?" "No." "There weren't any conditions. I did as much as I could."

"I wish winter wouldn't come yet." "That's what it looked like? It's you in this picture?"
"I don't know. No, it's not me. I was never there."

The problem wasn't only medical. The children didn't cry because they didn't learn how./ the pedagogical experts were missing.

A voice. 1ˢᵗ Commentary:
"I'm bothered the most not by the horrible acts at the time, but by your trying to implant in people's conscience the same logic used by the old regime: the one who's a legionary is a murderer, and, implicitly, his killing is justified. Such thinking led to the political victims of the old regime. There will be enough people to do as you please. Will you be happy then?"

A voice. 2ⁿᵈ Commentary:
"Eugenics in itself is not a bad thing, as long as it's a personal option, and not a state policy implemented as a criminal measure. It's a big difference aborting on request of a fetus affected by the Down syndrome, or another severe malformation, and the deliberate extermination of individuals affected by the same disease, as a state policy, cruelly imposed. Many western countries, among them the USA, Canada, and Sweden implemented public policies of sterilization of the undesirable individuals until the '70s.
These facts raised an enormous scandal."

4. Retrocession

The formation of the Self is symbolized in a dream by a fortress or a stadium—a fenced interior yard surrounded by swamps or garbage, dividing it into two opposite areas where the subject struggles to reach the far, imposing castle, the shape of which (sometimes present in the same scenario) symbolizes the identity in an amazing way.

*

For the building, Tisza Gheorghe and Tisza Coloman asked for one million euros, and for the entire property, 1.5 million euros.

"Maintaining the buildings in the use of the Bihor General Directorate for Assistance and Social Protection and the Bihor Protective Child Services through the Center for the Recuperation and Rehabilitation for Handicapped Persons Cighid is justified by the fact that 66 handicapped persons are still enrolled in this institution. Promoting and respecting the rights of the persons with handicap fall mainly under the jurisdiction of the local public administration where the person with handicap resides or lives, and, to a lesser degree, under the central public administration, civil society, and the family or the legal representative of the person with handicap."

5. The last trace

In the end, there will be no trace,
as if the prints could exist as a clue;
no trace is ultimately a sign without trace.
It will appear somewhere, surrounding us.
Nothing outside, nothing inside.

But when the sunset draws near, at a distance so short you could
touch it,
its redness drips over the world full of shards
and flesh.

For one moment, nothing is felt. Only the shadows are seen,
trembling in the gradually diminishing light.

Conclusions

But let's not forget:

The man loves the woman and the woman loves the man.
The product of their love is the child, loved by the man and the woman.
The state loves the man, who loves the woman, who loves.
The proof of the love between these three is, as mentioned, the children.

The State, and the man, and the woman love the child madly.
For this, they created the family.
The family was the small motherland,/ As motherland was the large family!

Since then, the State loves the motherland, as much as the man loves the woman.
And they all love each other!

Epode: Run. Be/come animal again again and again, with no end.

Instead of selective bibliography

The following also participated in the writing of this post-study:
Ion Popescu, the grandfather of the scribe,
then:

HEIDEGGER Himself
The Natural Buffon, The Unrivalled Platon,
Mr. Isidor de Sevilla and Mr. Otto Weininger
Goethe the Poet, some Melville
The Ailing Rousseau, Saint Sade
One Deleuze & Two Guattari, Derrida
Gellu and Lyggia, Alexei Vakulovski, voices
Texts: Michelle Calka, Sherry Turkle, Peter-Paul Verbeek
Doctors: Petrini de Galatz, Dumitru D. Velicu, etc.
Three ladies: Anemone Latzina, Linda Ashear, Sarah Kofman
Others: CTP (Cristian Tudor Popescu), people
Plus a few websites already mentioned in the text.
Not to forget the all-important contribution of the eternal-useful-usable EXD[1].
Lastly, special thanks to Mr. Stalin and Mr. Hitler, without whom this post-research study not only wouldn't be possible, but it wouldn't make any sense.

Warm thanks to all!

---

[1]EXD=Explained Dictionary of the Romanian Language

Acknowledgments

Grateful acknowledgments from both the translator and author are made to the editors of the following journals and presses where groups of poems from this collection first appeared, sometimes in earlier versions:

A selection of poems titled *About Death* was published in Alchemy.

The entire section *Punch! And They Bit* was published in *Asymptote.*

The entire section *The beast, or about hunger. The second seizure* was published in *AzonaL.*

Selections from the section *This Is Not a Poem* were published in *Barzakh Magazine.*

The entire section *Experiment! Experiment!* was published in *Bateau Literary Magazine.*

The section *This Is Not a Poem* was selected as the Editors' Pick for National Poetry Month and published by Brain Mill Press in April 2019.

The poems *The bird, or about flying. The first seizure* and *Impression from Olympus* were published in Bourgeon in a special issue celebrating Women in Translation Month, 2019.

A selection of poems titled *Space* was published in *Brooklyn Rail/ In Translation.*

The poems *Promenade, The perforated space, Sad-ism*, and *The collectivization of the voice* were published in *Burrow Press Review.*

The entire section *The bird, or about flying. The first seizure* was published in *Entropy.*

Selections from the manuscript were published in *RHINO*.

*

The original Romanian language version of this book, *Confiscarea bestiei (o postcercetare)*, was published by frACTalia Press in 2016.

The Spanish translation of this book, *La privación de la bestia (una investigación post-facto),* was published by Ediciones Hasta Trilce, Buenos Aires, Argentina, in 2021.

About the Author

Iulia Militaru is a writer and editor of frACTalia Press, as well as a member of the collectives Literature and Feminism and Workshop X. She has authored: *Marea pipeadă* (*The Great Pipe Epic*, 2010), *dramadoll* (co-authored with Anca Bucur and Cristina Florentina Budar in 2012), *Confiscarea bestiei (o postcercetare)* (*The Seizure of the Beast. A Post-research*, 2016), and *Atlas (auto)matIon (auto)BIO/graphy/I© de câteva tipuri principale de discursuri* (*Atlas (auto)matIon (auto)BIO/graphy/I© of several main types of speeches*, e-book in 2017; second edition in print, 2019). She published poems digital collages in several international journals, as well as a theoretic study, *Metaforic și metonimic: o tipologie a poeziei* (*Metaphorical and Metonymical: a Typology of Poetry*, 2011). Interested in the New Materialism and the Queer Theory, in 2018 she started working on the project Maia Şerbănescu to imagine new forms of material existence, alternative sexualities, and corporeal transformations when immersed in different environments. Maia Şerbănescu is a hybrid xeno-entity fascinated by *ero guro nansensu* and *gurlesque poetry*, and the author of collections *Fuck off, Mr. Charcot!* (2019) și *OikosLogia. Ştiinţa casei socialiste și a fiinţelor posibile* (OikosLogia. *The Science of the Socialist House and of the Possible Beings*, 2022). In 2020, she published the first volume of her research, *Literatura și fenomenul alienării* (*Literature and the Phenomenon of Alienation*), a thorough study on the way the concept of alienation was produced in the 19th century in Romania and on the realities generated by its network of significations.

About the Translator

Claudia Serea is a Romanian-American poet, translator, and editor. Her poems and translations are published in *Field, New Letters, Prairie Schooner, The Malahat Review, The Puritan, Oxford Poetry*, among others. Serea won a Pushcart Prize, the Joanne Scott Kennedy Memorial Prize from the Poetry Society of Virginia, and the *New Letters* Readers Award for her poems. Her poems have been translated in Russian, French, Italian, Arabic, and Farsi, and have been featured on *The Writer's Almanac*.

She is the author of seven poetry collections and four chapbooks, most recently *In Those Years, No One Slept* (Broadstone Books, 2023) and *Writing on the Walls at Night* (Unsolicited Press, 2022). Her collection of poems translated into Arabic, *Tonight I'll Become a Lake into which You'll Sink*, was published in Cairo, Egypt, in 2021.

Serea is a founding editor of National Translation Month, and she co-edited and co-translated *The Vanishing Point That Whistles, an Anthology of Contemporary Romanian Poetry* (Talisman House Publishing, 2011). She also translated from Romanian Adina Dabija's *Beautybeast* (Northshore Press, 2012).

Claudia Serea serves on the board of The Red Wheelbarrow Poets and is one of the curators of the Red Wheelbarrow Poetry Readings. She writes, translates, and edits manuscripts in Rutherford, New Jersey.

FSC
www.fsc.org

MIX
Paper
FSC® C100212

Printed by Imprimerie Gauvin
Gatineau, Québec